Forgotten faces of Neath & Port Talbot

By David Roberts

www.bryngoldbooks.com

First published in Great Britain in 2010
by Bryngold Books Ltd.,
100 Brynau Wood, Cimla,
Neath, South Wales SA11 3YQ.

www.bryngoldbooks.com

Typesetting, layout,
editing and design
by Bryngold Books

Copyright © David Roberts 2010

All rights reserved. No part of this publication may be reproduced, stored in a retrieval system, or transmitted in any form, or by any means, electronic, mechanical, photocopying, recording, or otherwise without the prior permission, in writing, of the copyright holder, nor be otherwise circulated in any form or binding or cover other than that in which it is published and without a similar condition being imposed on the subsequent publisher.

ISBN 978-1-905900-18-3

**Printed and bound
in Wales by
Gomer Press,
Llandysul, Ceredigion.**

Contents

Appreciation	4
Foreword	5
Compendium of change	6
Street scene	7
Familiar faces	47
District diary	61
Guiding lights	77
Younger days	87
The entertainers	95
School report	109
Moving along	125
Break time	137
Working ways	147
Party time	161
Sports view	175

Appreciation

Forgotten faces of Neath & Port Talbot is a book, like all those before, that would not have been possible without the assistance of many people. Among them are my wife Cheryl, for her ceaseless behind the scenes support; Anthony Isaac, Neil Melbourne, John Vivian Hughes, John & Barbara Southard, Colin Scott and Steven H Jones, who have all helped in so many different ways. Then there are those who once again, have shared so many delightful photographs. Among them Tony & Hilary Llewellyn, Janice Austin, Robert Jones, Ieuan & Dorothy Jones, the late Ken Kingdom, EJ Cross, John Newman, Roger and Veronica Gale, Bob & Ann Merchant, Val Thomas, Ken Rees, Mike Hopkins, Eileen Cottey, Keith & Ann Davies, Alun & Kay Rees, T G Evans, Teresa Cummings, Anne Brown, George Evans, Bill & Jean Lewis, Peter Ryan, John & Eira Beynon, Steve Dinham, Christine Basten, Bill Barton, Brian Harry, Bill Adams, George Vincent, Steve Pitman, Norman Evans, Margaret O'Connor, Angela Locke, David Edwards, Mrs D Jones, David Jones, Enid Farrell, John Matthews, Geoffrey Nicholas, Colin Walters, Gwyn John, the late Denys Parsons, Helen Smith, Port Talbot Library, the late Harry Humphries, Kester Reason, Anne Morgan, Carol Rainford, Elaine Wise, Margaret & Tony Rowlands, Rosemary Matthews, Morris Fish, Eunice Hunter Rowe, Brian Harry, Marie Hopkins, Malcolm & Mary Rees, Terry Knipe, Lucy King, Rosemary Matthews, Roger Needs, Terry Davies, Jean & Colin Griffiths, Allun Davies, Mrs Andrews, Anne Pearlman, Viv & Susan Roberts, Chris Griffiths, Enid Jones, Malcolm Wiltshire, Fred Harris, Steve & Lee Watkins, David Richards, Mrs L Lamner, Mike Hoile, David Davies, Stan Thomas, Aileen Buckingham, Mrs Thomas, Fred Archer, Wyndham Griffiths, Mary Roberts, the late Vincent Thomas, Chris & Paul Rowlands, Allen Morgans, Robert Thomas, Mrs D Morris, Linda Feltham, Rev Peter Jenkins, June Shakeshaft, Jeff Huckeridge and Robert Deakin. We are also grateful to those whose photographs may not have been selected for this book, purely on the grounds of space. Their part has been just as invaluable. My thanks go to you all.

Share your pictures

You too, can play a part in recording the history of your area by contributing photographs to the next Neath & Port Talbot nostalgia book. Please telephone 01639 643961 or e-mail david.roberts@bryngoldbooks.com to discover the ways in which you can do this. We would be delighted to hear from you. All photographs, black and white or colour, of people, places, events, streets, buildings, schooldays and sport are considered whatever their age, subject or format. They are all promptly returned. Also, if you have missed any of the previous 11 books then contact us now as some titles are still available. You can also check out our web site at
www.bryngoldbooks.com
for details of our other fascinating local nostalgia books.

Foreword

Congratulations David!

Yet another beautiful book illustrating recent and past times of Neath Port Talbot. It is without doubt one that can be enjoyed by people of all ages.

Pictures of many aspects of life for the older reader to enjoy and reminisce over, perhaps some will even recognise themselves, their family or friends in the street parties or school pictures. At the same time younger readers will enjoy learning and knowing how their grandparents lived, worked and played.

Forgotten faces of Neath & Port Talbot is about local history, about yesterday and yesteryear, and it leaves me in no doubt that community spirit is still very much alive in the valleys and towns of the County Borough of Neath Port Talbot.

Thank you David for such a wonderful book and best wishes for all that may follow in the future.

Councillor Lella James
Mayor of Neath Port Talbot
August, 2010.

Compendium of change

Time and tide they say, wait for no man — or woman. How true that statement is when we consider that we are already at the end of the first decade of the 21st Century. It has been a period which, for better or worse, has brought a heady mix of changes, some good, others not so, to our proud county borough.

The past year alone brought the devastating fire which destroyed the Aquadome leisure complex on Aberavon Beach. Scores will recall spending happy hours there in its early days as the Afan Lido and for them the pictures of that era in *Forgotten faces of Neath & Port Talbot* will be tinged with sadness. But that same year has also brought more positive developments. Among them the announcement of massive investment in the future of the Corus steel plant. There's clear evidence too of the re-emergence of Neath's historic Gwyn Hall, a much missed landmark and venue, something that can only be welcomed. Like the Afan Lido, it had long played a part in the lives of the communities around them and are examples of how change can manifest itself. Many other facets of our daily lives have come and gone in that time. They may not figure as significantly on the urban landscape, but they are equally important.

People and faces change too. While some residents leave the area, they are often replaced by new residents. Those to whom we may have said farewell, might still make their presence felt on the pages of this book.

Forgotten faces of Neath & Port Talbot offers a fresh harvest of pictorial memories each one ensuring a revival of one long forgotten moment or another. As always, people, places and events occupy a big part in this photographic compendium. That's because all three play a big part in the bread and butter history of our towns and our county borough that unfolds each day.

The images on the following pages will remind some of schoolday friendships, others of events they were proud to attend or take part in; they also offer the opportunity to reminisce; to recall long forgotten work colleagues or escapades on distant days out. This year the Guide movement marks its centenary. The important part its members have played in the life of Neath and Port Talbot is reflected in a chapter dedicated to saluting their exploits and their achievements.

Forgotten faces of Neath & Port Talbot is a peoples' record of our ordinary everyday lives. It is the people who have provided the images. This means memories can be shared and undoubtedly reflects the existence of a true community spirit. That is ample reason to treasure the look back in time that this book affords. While the towns of Neath and Port Talbot move forward it allows us to refresh our memories of the way they once were.

David Roberts,
2010

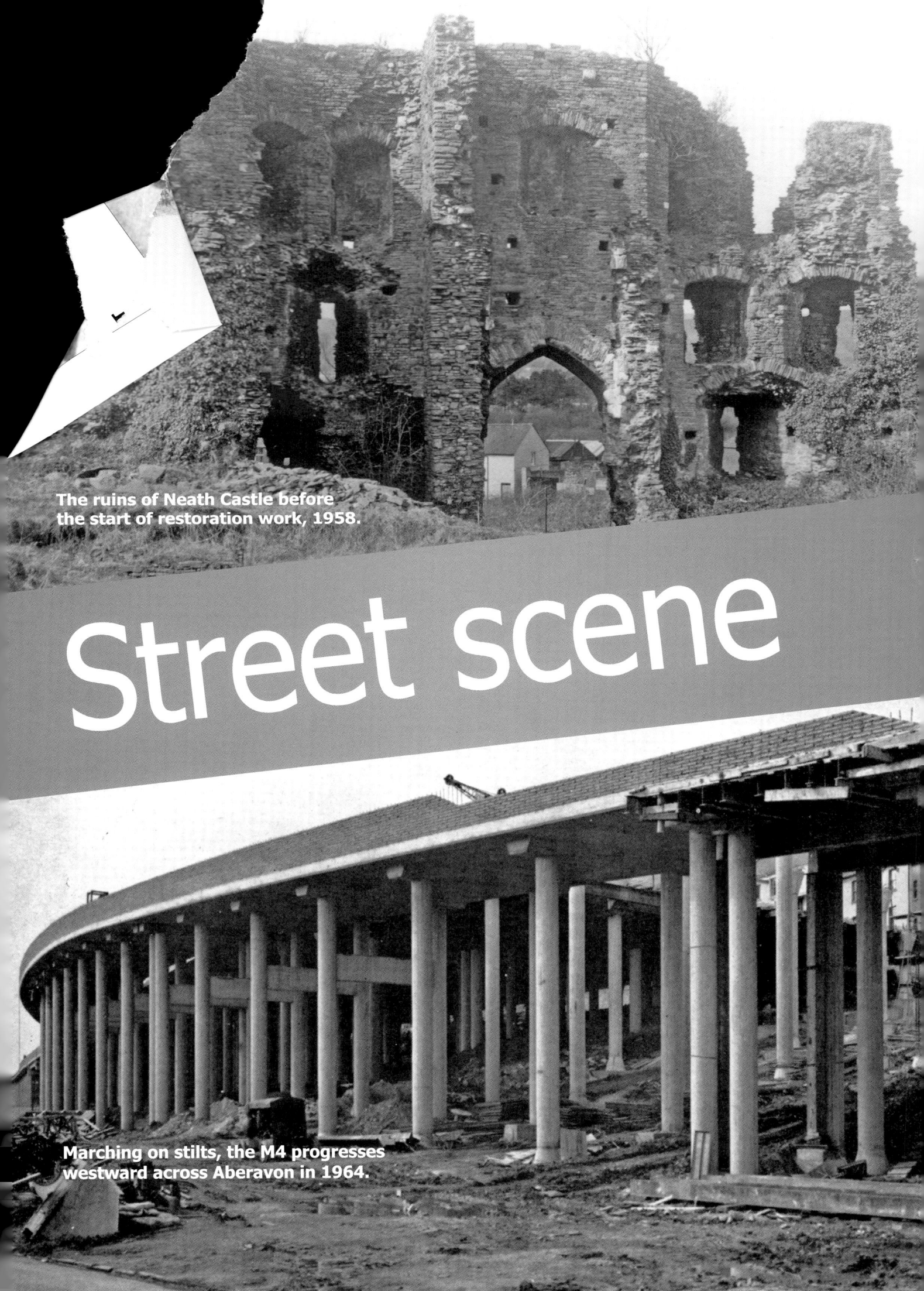

The ruins of Neath Castle before the start of restoration work, 1958.

Street scene

Marching on stilts, the M4 progresses westward across Aberavon in 1964.

The imposing Walnut Tree Hotel stands proudly at the junction of High Street and Water Street, Aberavon, 1903.

The Cambrian Hotel, at the junction of Windsor Road and Alfred Street, Neath, 1903.

This fascinating panorama of Port Talbot captured in 1930 shows a scene far different to that which exists today.

The forecourt of Neath General railway station in the late 1920s. The buses were operated by the Great Western Railway to connect its services with outlying districts.

Shops of all kinds, from a barbers to a provisions merchant line both sides of Water Street as the photographer points his camera towards its junction with High Street, Aberavon, in 1900.

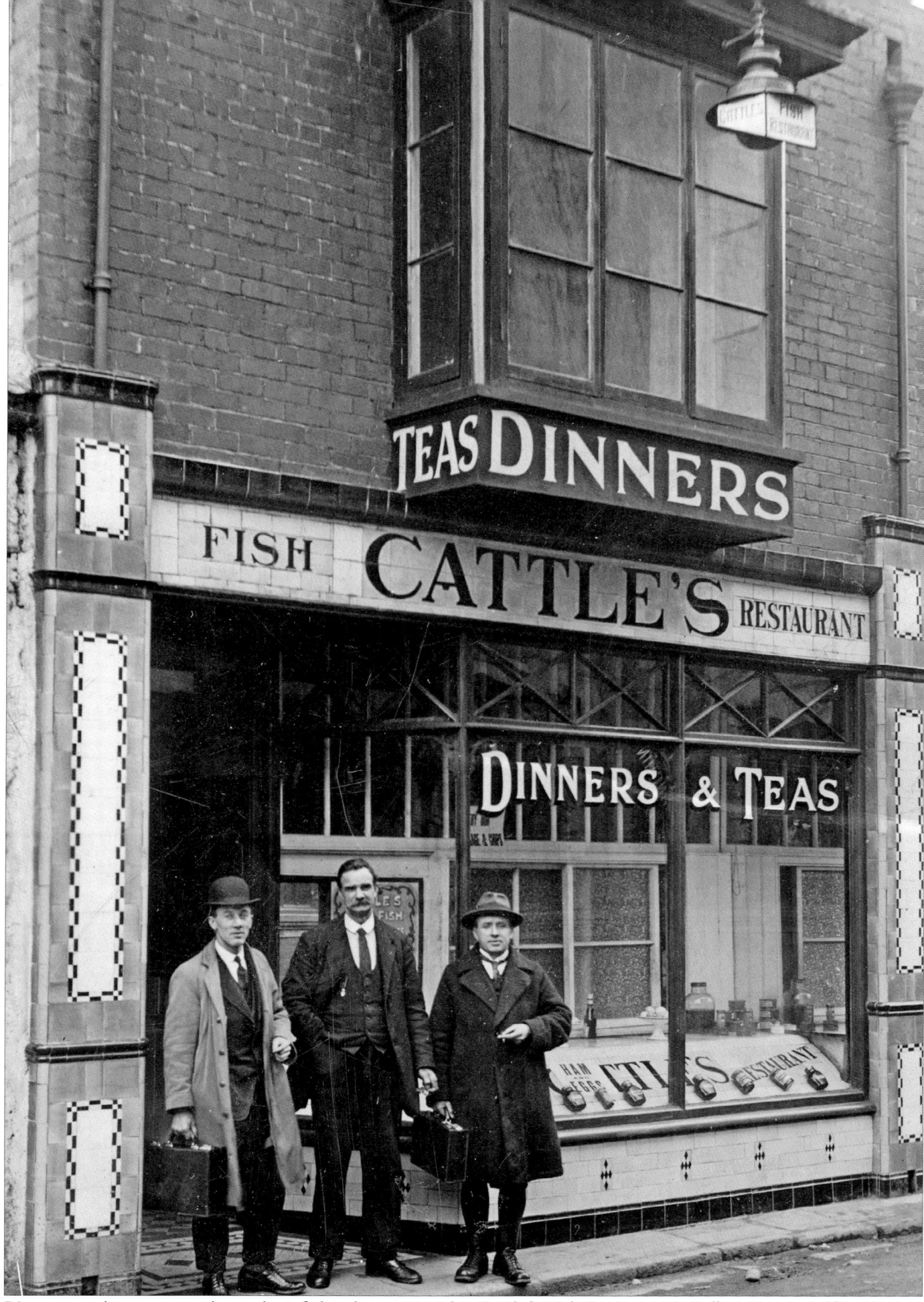

Dinners and teas were the order of the day at popular Cattle's Fish Restaurant, Talbot Square, Aberavon. Proprietor Mr Cattle is seen with two colleagues, outside the main entrance, late 1930s.

The Mechanics' Institute, Church Place, Neath, early 1950s. For some years it housed the town's museum. The graveyard of St Thomas's parish church is in the foreground.

Saron Chapel, Penycae Road, Port Talbot, early 1950s.

Water Street, Aberavon, with St Joseph's Roman Catholic Church in the background, late 1940s.

Two gentlemen, Mr Harris, left and Mr Morgan, take a break on a bench in Victoria Gardens, Neath in the mid-1950s. The town's library is in the background.

Looking down Wind Street, Neath, from its junction with Water Street, 1977. The Shakespeare Inn is on the right and the Ancient Briton in the distance. The majority of the buildings here were demolished to make way for the town's Tesco store, latterly occupied by the Wilkinsons company.

Looking down the Beach Hill, Aberavon, along Victoria Road towards the sea, late 1940s. The Vivian Hotel on the right has now been demolished and replaced with new homes.

Queen Street, Neath, 1960 showing demolition of Borough stores. Built about 1842 it was once the headquarters of Neath Philosophical Society, housing a library, reading room and observatory.

The Castle Hotel, The Parade, Neath, 1955.

Capel Moriah, The Causeway, Aberavon, early 1950s.

Looking eastwards along High Street, Port Talbot, towards the Walnut Tree Hotel, 1965. Before long all of the buildings in this picture would be demolished to make way for town centre redevelopment.

Looking across the River Neath in 1962 towards Gillard's garage, built on the site of the Leather House, Bridge Street, Neath. At the time the bridge to the left was the main northern traffic artery for the town.

Orchard Street, Neath, November 1968. The MC Cafe, between the mini-market and gents' outfitter Louis Zeiler was a popular meeting place. The Gwyn Hall is on the right and Victoria Gardens to the left.

Vivian Square, Aberavon, looking towards Wern Street, early 1950s. The roofline of Wern Chapel is just visible on the top left.

Albert James's sweet and pram shop in the Aberavon shopping arcade, early 1950s. The shop was also a good target for anyone looking to buy a tricycle or bicycle too!

The junction of Greenway Road with London Road, Neath, 1967. London Road Presbyterian Church, is on the right and the shop, then a hair stylists is now a Co-operative pharmacy.

The Bird in Hand field, Neath, early 1960s. The former fairground was donated by Sir David Evans Bevan as a site for a building to house both the Borough and Rural District councils.

Talbot Road, Port Talbot looking towards the town centre, 1955. The former Labour Exchange is on the right.

Edmund Harris and Peter Evans in Florence Street, Neath, proudly showing off the Austin Mini car which belonged to Fred Harris 1967. The old Maria Street Chapel is in the background.

Shops in High Street, Aberavon, alongside the Walnut Tree Hotel, 1959.

Maesycwrt Terrace, Port Talbot looking towards its junction with Abbey Road, mid-1950s. The entrance to the town's Memorial Park and St Theodore's Church are both on the right.

The building behind this impromtu 1968 Neath car park had a number of uses before becoming the Moose Hall. It was a Methodist Church, Catholic Church, and ambulance depot at various times.

The boarded up building of Neath Riverside station, a relic of the Neath and Brecon Railway, off Bridge Street, 1968.

The view down Forge Road towards Bethany Square, Port Talbot, mid-1950s.

The entrance to the shopping arcade that existed below Port Talbot's Municipal Buildings, flanked by two of the town's once popular retailers, late 1950s. The building was demolished to make way for town centre redevelopment in 1972.

Only one side of Florence Street, Neath, remains after the other was demolished to make way for construction of the town's congestion relieving southern link road, early 1960s.

Demolition of houses at Pentyla, Aberavon, prior to town centre redevelopment and construction of the M4 flyover, early 1960s.

Orchard Street, Neath, before the start of demotion to make way for an extension to the town's Woolworth's store, 1966. Poundland and Argos are now here.

The former Neath Riverside station of the Neath & Brecon Railway just off the town's Bridge Street, 1968.

Church Lane, Aberavon, 1964. The buildings here were demolished in 1972 to make way for town centre redevelopment.

A panorama of Port Talbot during construction of the M4 motorway, September 1965.

High Street, Aberavon, looking east, 1967.

These stores stood on the site of Neath's main post office, Windsor Road, until the late 1960s.

The Gnoll Brook, Neath, had been a source of worry at times of heavy rain for many years. An interceptor drain using 78 inch diameter concrete pipes was laid in 1968 taking the brook underground along Forster Road, the former Gnoll School yard, past the civic centre, through the fairground and into the River Neath. One of the pipes is shown framing the civic centre with an obliging youngster standing inside, during 1968.

The lodge and gatehouse of the Gnoll House that stood on the bend on Cimla Road, 1965. It was later demolished and replaced by a detached house.

Water Street Baptist Chapel, Water Street, Aberavon, late 1960s.

Aberavon Working Men's Club, Talbot Square, Aberavon, mid-1960s. The alleyway on the left side of the building led to the New Hall.

Neath's main Post Office, Windsor Road, 1968. The original Post Office is on the left and the new building was later extended to what can be seen today.

The towers of St Mary's Parish Church and Port Talbot's municipal buildings are visible in this view of demolition at Water Street, 1971. The roof of the former Aberavon market is on the left.

Water Street, Neath, near its junction with Wind Street, 1968. The two pubs in the foregound, the George & Dragon and Shakespeare Inn have long gone, but the Duke of Wellington, in the distance survives. The once popular Hole in the Wall restaurant can also be seen across the junction.

STREET SCENE

Shops in Queen Street, Neath, including the town's newly extended Marks & Spencer store, 1969.

Derelict shops and the exterior of Aberavon Market, Water Street, Aberavon, 1968. They were demolished some years later.

Ropewalk Terrace, off Windsor Road, Neath March 2, 1969. The bridge on the left carries the main Paddington to Swansea railway line.

Talbot Square, Port Talbot, once a bustling area became a car park during Port Talbot town centre redevelopment, 1971.

STREET SCENE

The Dock Hotel, Aberavon, 1972.

Two telephone kiosks stand sentinel at a deserted Victoria Gardens bus station, Neath during a wintry day in February, 1969.

Aberavon Market after demolition of buildings that stood on the opposite side of Water Street, including the Railway Tavern, Smith & May's chemists and Thorne's paint and wallpaper shop, 1972.

The Magistrates Court at Water Street, Neath, under construction during July 1976

STREET SCENE

A Creamline Services bus collects passengers at Victoria Gardens bus station in the shadow of St David's Church, Neath, 1981. Traffic can be seen flowing in the opposite direction to that of today.

Looking across Talbot Square, Aberavon, late 1960s. Now only Ebenezer Chapel, on the right, survives.

The scene in Gnoll Park Road, Neath, after a heavy overnight snow fall, 1983.

The Causeway steps, Aberavon, 1972. They originally led from High Street, towards Springfield and the Mountain Schools. The schools were demolished to facilitate construction of the M4 motorway.

STREET SCENE

The Halfpenny bridge across the River Afan at Aberavon, 1972.

Work underway on the creation of fast food outlet Dollar Burger at Briton Ferry Road, Neath, late 1970s. All the buildings here were later demolished to make way for new housing.

An interesting north-westerly view across Neath town centre over the rooftops of the town's Hillside district. Taken in the summer of 1983, it shows that much of the retail and roadway development at the northern fringe had yet to begin.

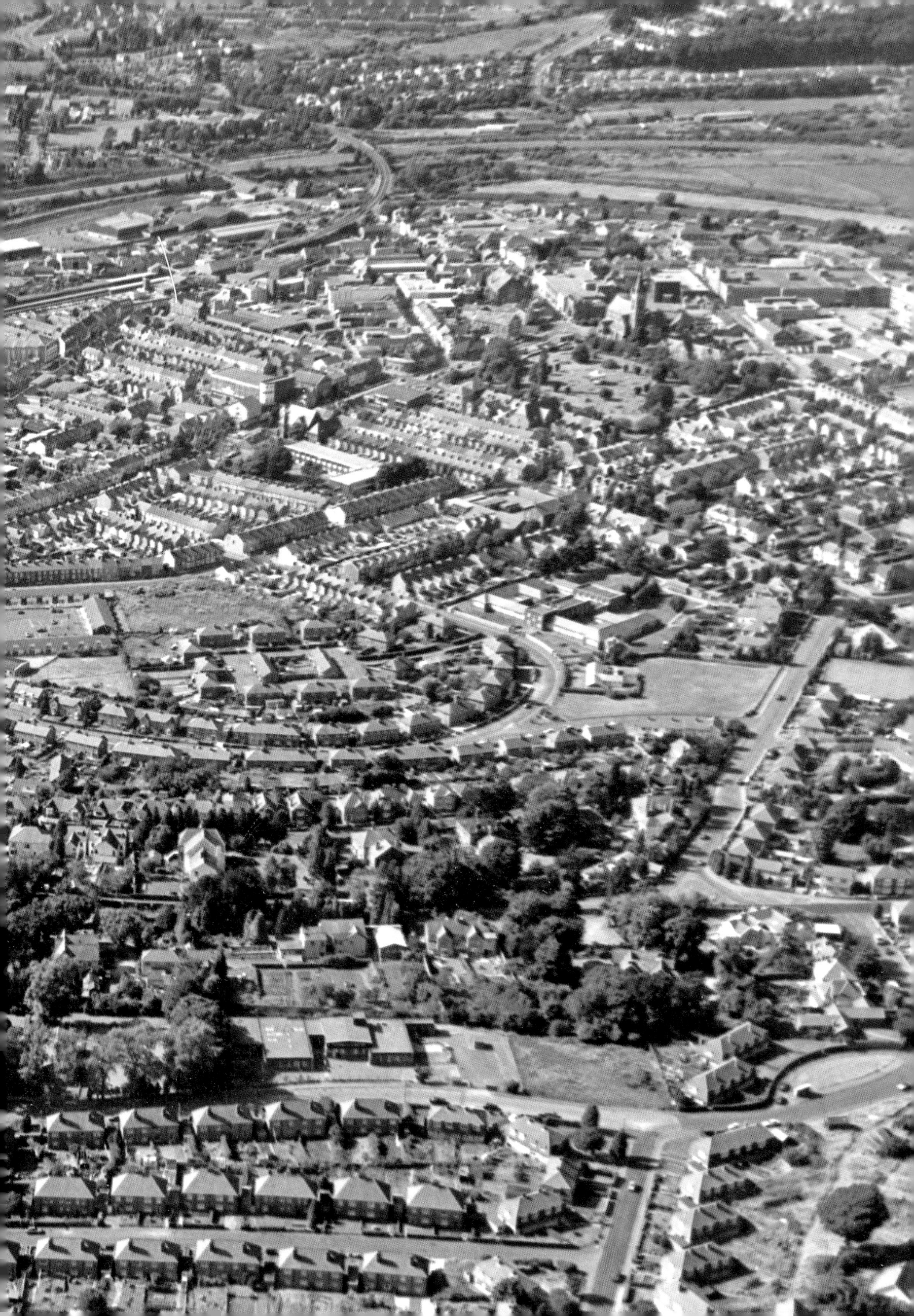

A view of James Street, Neath, 1988. It vanished under town centre redevelopment. Morrisons supermarket and smaller retail units occupy this site now.

Aberafan Shopping Centre, 1981. Both the stores on either side of this view looking towards the main square have now vanished from the high street, nationwide.

Traffic waits patiently for the passing of a train at the level crossing alongside Port Talbot railway station, during the mid-1970s.

Swans on Neath Canal at Bridge Street, Neath, 1987.

There was little traffic in Broad Street, Port Talbot, or anywhere else in the town after a heavy snowfall in January 1982.

A view across the James Street redevelopment area, Neath, on August 25, 1988, showing the former offices of accountants Watkins Bradfield. This area is now the car park of Morrison's supermarket.

Familiar faces

A group of men outside the New Hall, Talbot Square, Aberavon, late 1930s.

Actress Jessie Matthews receives a presentation from staff at Phillips Bros department store, The Square, Neath, on a visit there, early 1950s.

Councillor William S Watkins, Mayor of Neath, at a presentation with his niece, Mrs Audrey Durnell as acting Mayoress, 1960.

Members of the Gooch family, of Rhanallt Street, Margam, Port Talbot, mid-1920s.

FAMILIAR FACES

Members of the social studies group of Neath Evening Townswomens' Guild during a trip to Spillers Flour Mill, Cardiff, late 1950s.

Members of the Humphries family of Neath in 1909. They are from the left: Henry, George, Mary and, standing, Mary Louisa.

A father and son stand outside their home in Elba Avenue, Margam, Port Talbot, during the Second World War.

Staff of Leslies Stores, Green Street, Neath, 1960.

Members and organisers of Pontrhydyfen Youth Club, early 1950s.

Patients and staff at Cimla Hospital, Neath, 1958.

Members of the Neath detachment of the Red Cross, late 1950s.

Family friends and residents of Mountain Row, Aberavon, gather for a golden wedding celebration, early 1950s.

FAMILIAR FACES

Members and organisers of Port Talbot Methodist Church youth club at a Christmas party, during the early 1950s.

The junior group of Melincrythan Amateur Operatic Society, 1967.

The organising committee of the 10th Port Talbot Scout group, late 1950s.

A presentation to a retiring senior operator at the Catalytic Reformer Plant at BP's Llandarcy refinery, Neath, early 1980s.

Officers, committee and guests of Neath RAFA Club at a presentation to a charity fund originally launched by the Mayor of Newport, 1980.

Members of the Young Wives group at St Paul's Church, Aberavon, 1960.

Some of those who attended the Senior Citizens group at the Welfare Hall, Cimla, during a trip to Great Yarmouth, 1968.

Prince Charles opens a community centre that was originally a pithead baths and ancillary buildings at Seven Sisters, late 1980s.

A gathering of residents at Park Street, Taibach, Port Talbot, early 1960s.

FAMILIAR FACES

Selina Jones, the landlady of the Vivian Hotel, Victoria Road, Aberavon, surrounded by regulars and friends at a presentation evening held there to mark her retirement, 1963.

A group of employees celebrating 25 years service at BP Llandarcy gathered around plant manager, Mr A Daniels, 1991.

Staff of Port Talbot Borough Council's engineering department relax with a drink at the town's Carlton Club, mid-1960s.

Retired Shell-Mex and BP fuel tanker drivers who until their retirement had worked at Llandarcy refinery, during a reunion in 2007. The company ceased operation in 1986.

FAMILIAR FACES

Chief guests, including Mayor and Mayoress of Neath Port Talbot, Councillor and Mrs Malcolm Jones, at the opening of a community centre at Resolven in 1999. The building had previously been the village's Salvation Army hall.

Mr Michael Ryan among colleagues who gathered to mark his retirement from the British Steel Corporation's Port Talbot plant, 1968. He had started work aged 14 in Port Talbot Steelworks.

Staff of FW Woolworth's store, Port Talbot, celebrate a colleague's long service in 1979.

Guests at a pensioners Christmas lunch at BP Llandarcy, December 1975.

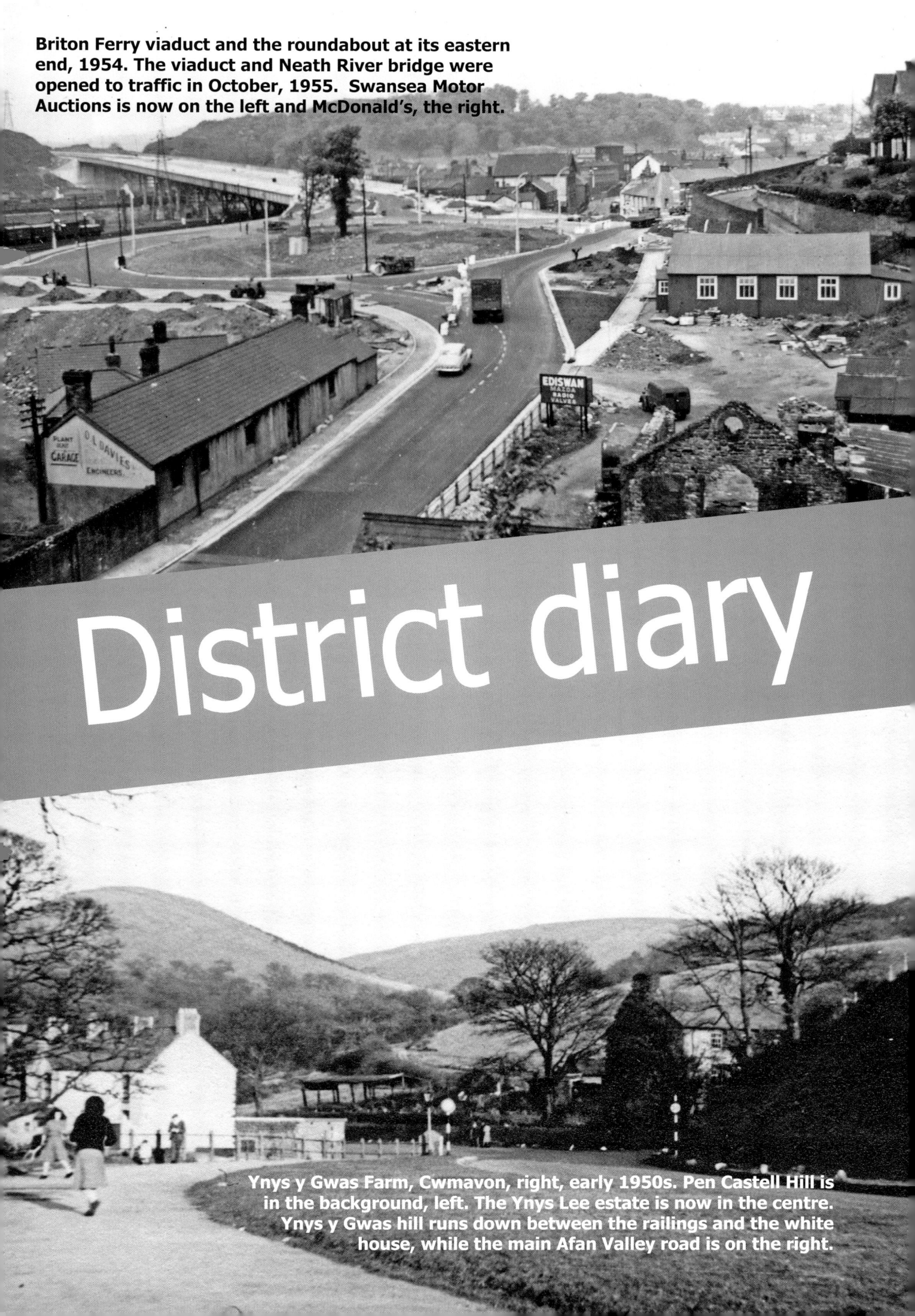

Briton Ferry viaduct and the roundabout at its eastern end, 1954. The viaduct and Neath River bridge were opened to traffic in October, 1955. Swansea Motor Auctions is now on the left and McDonald's, the right.

District diary

Ynys y Gwas Farm, Cwmavon, right, early 1950s. Pen Castell Hill is in the background, left. The Ynys Lee estate is now in the centre. Ynys y Gwas hill runs down between the railings and the white house, while the main Afan Valley road is on the right.

The railway station at Neath Abbey, 1952.

Richmond House, Taibach with Caradoc Street behind, 1920. The mountainside houses have long since vanished with the arrival of the M4 motorway.

The Alexandra Restaurant, Aberavon Beach, was a hive of activity on May 23, 1902. This was the date of the official opening of the first section of the nearby seafront promenade. Later the restaurant became known as the New Alex Grill and today it is still a popular restaurant rendezvous known as Bar Gallois.

Cimla Bach Farm, Resolven, 1920s.

The ruins of Neath Abbey, 1950.

Looking across the plant nurseries of Baglan Hall, early 1930s. This is now Baglan Park.

Baglan Home Farm, which was part of the Baglan Hall estate, early 1930s. It later housed the growing community's first library.

Etberne Grange, later known as Court Herbert House, Neath, prior to demolition, late 1960s. It was a former grange of Neath Abbey.

A young man and his dog pose for the camera alongside the South Wales Mineral Railway track, 1943. Behind them, the village of Tonmawr.

Afan Valley Close, Cimla, Neath, after heavy snow in January, 1983.

The nurses' home at Neath General Hospital, Penrhiwtyn, 1987.

Looking along Victoria Road, Aberavon, from the beach towards town, late 1940s.

Looking across Sandfields from the sand dunes of Little Warren towards Baglan, early 1950. Most of the properties in the distance are prefabs. Victoria Road is in the foreground and Tywyn School stands alongside these houses now.

Blocks of flats at the Saltings, Briton Ferry, 1968. The playground contained a selection of large scale concrete animals.

The view from gardens of now demolished houses in Walters Road, Melyn, Neath, early 1970s. The Baglan Engineering Company's works is in the centre and the old Melyn school, on the right.

Albert James in his sweet kiosk outside the Jersey Beach Hotel, Aberavon Beach, mid-1950s. The young boy is possibly his grandson Philip.

Looking over Velindre and Trefelin Secondary School, early 1950s.

A lock on the Neath Canal at Resolven, early 1990s.

Three curious schoolboys take a close look at early progress on construction of the sea wall and promenade at Aberavon Beach, 1955.

The boarded-up former primary school at Tonna, Neath, looks forlorn as it awaits demolition, 1994.

Work underway on demolishing one of Neath's oldest and most historic churches at Aberdulais to make way for the A465 dual carriageway. Aberdulais Baptist Church was built in 1849. The final service was held there on January 17, 1994.

Local authority housing at Cwmavon, early 1960s. Heol Mabon is in the centre, viewed from nearby Brynheulog Terrace.

Shops at The Square, off Main Road, Crynant, 1995.

Beulah Chapel in the centre of Groes village, Margam, being dismantled brick-by-brick in 1975 before its reconstruction in nearby Tollgate Park, where it re-opened in April 1976. The remainder of the village, 21 houses and a school, was demolished to make way for the M4 motorway.

An aerial view of BP's Llandarcy refinery and the surrounding area, late 1990s.

Demolition of the former Cimla Court Hotel, 77 Cimla Road, Neath during July, 2008.

An atmospheric view down the Afan Valley of the mining villages of Abergwynfi and Blaengwynfi, late 1970s. Avon colliery was formerly in the foreground.

DISTRICT DIARY

Abercregan Junior School, now demolished, early 1990s.

Looking along Afan Way, Port Talbot, as work progresses on the demolition of the Beach Hill road bridge 2006.

The railway bridge at Velindre, Port Talbot, mid-1950s.

An aerial view across Port Talbot showing the docks and land soon to be developed, early 1990s.

The year was 1988 and this was Neath's first out of town store. Madeley's DIY had a shop in Wind Street in the town centre before moving to this purpose-built 30,000 square feet store at Neath Abbey. The premises is now the home of Trade Centre Wales car supermarket.

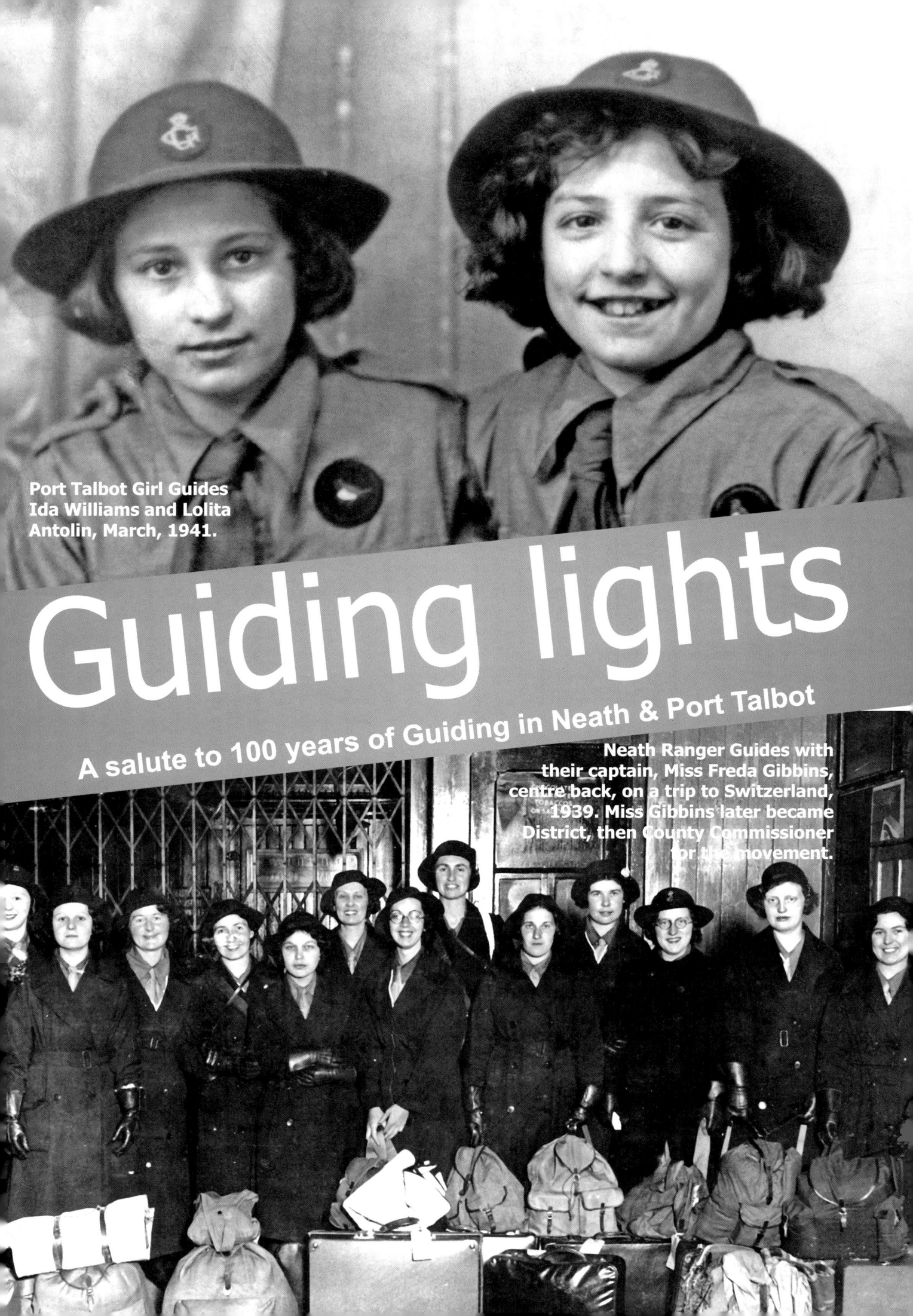

Port Talbot Girl Guides Ida Williams and Lolita Antolin, March, 1941.

Guiding lights

A salute to 100 years of Guiding in Neath & Port Talbot

Neath Ranger Guides with their captain, Miss Freda Gibbins, centre back, on a trip to Switzerland, 1939. Miss Gibbins later became District, then County Commissioner for the movement.

Members of the 1st Neath Guide Company with Ray Charles, centre, as captain, 1950s.

Neath Guides at camp in Penrice, Oxwich, 1937.

Neath Rangers with their leaders during a civic parade through the town, 1964.

Rest hour in camp for these Guides who were members of the 3rd Port Talbot (St Theodore's) Company, 1961. They were at Coedarhydyglyn, Vale of Glamorgan, at the time.

Members of the 3rd Port Talbot (St Theodore's) Guide Company during a Thinking Day event, 1962.

Members of the 3rd Port Talbot Guide Company packing boxes of donations for Oxfam, 1962.

Guides and their leaders on parade at Aberavon Beach, 1967.

Welsh Guides display their Duke of Edinburgh Gold Award certificates after receiving them at Buckingham Palace, London, 1970. Among them was Christine Hopkins from the 1st Port Talbot Land Rangers.

Members of the Swallow patrol of the 1st Aberavon Guides take a break during a camp, 1980.

A group of Guides gets stuck in Billy bashing at a summer camp, 1995.

Members of the 1st Baglan Guides on a carnival float, 1985. The carnival, in Swansea, was to celebrate 75 years of the movement. Every unit in the county was represented.

Members of the 1st Bryncoch, Neath, Guide Company at Land's End, Cornwall, during their summer camp, 1974.

Young Judith Shakeshaft is congratulated by fellow members of the 1st Aberavon Guide Company on receiving her Patrol Camp Permit, 1980.

Lady Baden Powell at the official opening of Neath Guide headquarters, June 1, 1964. With her on the right is Miss Freda Gibbins, County Commissioner.

Civic hospitality from Mayor and Mayoress of the Borough of Afan, Councillor and Mrs Raymond Morgan, at Port Talbot Civic Centre, for a group of visiting Guides from Denmark, August, 1983.

Neath and Port Talbot Guides joined by visiting overseas counterparts at County Hall, Swansea during West Glamorgan Guides' International Camp at Margam, 1983. They were given a civic welcome by Chairman of West Glamorgan County Council, Councillor Tom Jones.

Members of the 1st Baglan Guide Company cooking at Parkmill Centre, 1991.

Baglan Guides and their leaders prepare to set off on a trip to Switzerland, August, 1987.

Mrs Jean Gale, Afan Valley Division Guide Commissioner presents Lisa Williams of the 3rd Port Talbot Company with her Queen's Guide badge, 1984. This was the last time this award was made in Port Talbot before the badge system changed.

This group of Guides was Walking for Wildlife at Afan Argoed Country Park, as part of a World Wildlife Fund initiative, 1995.

Younger days

Two Neath youngsters all set for a trip into town, with their mum, early 1950s.

Bathtime 1950s style for this Port Talbot youngster.

Bathtime in a bowl for this new Port Talbot arrival in the early 1950s.

A trio of Melincrythan lads, smartly dressed in their Sunday best, 1938.

Some of the children of Tom and Margaret Reason of Skewen, in 1917. Tom played for Neath RFC from 1902-1912. From left, standing are: Arthur, William and Gladys; seated are: Louise, Ivor and Olive.

YOUNGER DAYS

A group of Scouts and Cubs at Cimla, 1954.

Youngsters of Abbots Close, Margam on the green near Groes, early 1960s. They were posing for a local newspaper photographer.

Members of the Salvation Army Childrens' Mission, Marshfield Road, Neath, with Peter Jenkins and his ventriloquists dummies, early 1950s.

Two Baglan children, smartly dressed for a visit to Neath's September Fair, 1966.

A back garden bathtub made an ideal impromptu pool for this Briton Ferry youngster, early 1950s.

YOUNGER DAYS

Three Port Talbot youngsters enjoy their lunch on a caravan holiday, early 1950s.

Youngsters at Giants Grave, Briton Ferry, mid-1950s.

Mayor of Afan, Councillor Elwyn Williams, dropped in on a story telling session during Children's week at Aberafan Shopping Centre, July 1979.

Three Cimla youngsters show off their new St John Ambulance Brigade uniforms, 1955.

YOUNGER DAYS

These four young girls from Ynysygerwn, Aberdulais, were dressed in traditional Welsh costume to celebrate St David's Day, March 1, 1962.

Goytre Youth Club members, at their annual party at Goytre Community Centre, Port Talbot, mid-1960s.

FORGOTTEN FACES OF **NEATH & PORT TALBOT**

Children enjoy some fun on the slide in the Gnoll grounds, Neath, 1954.

A helping hand from mum for this young girl in Dock Street, Aberavon, late 1940.

A Port Talbot girl in her Christmas fairy finery, 1953.

Two young boys play on the lawn of a house in Old Road, Baglan, 1963.

The Brython Glee Singers, of Briton Ferry, 1906.

The entertainers

The Boro' Paraders jazz band, Port Talbot, with an array of trophies, 1936.

The cast of Aberavon and Port Talbot Amateur Operatic Society's production of the Mikado, 1920.

Members of a concert party at Gnoll Secondary Modern School, 1954.

Members of Pontrhydyfen and District Temperance Band, complete with instruments, 1931.

This group of chorus girls took part in an operatic production of Rebel Maid by Afan and District Operatic Society, at The Old Empire, Talbot Road, Port Talbot, 1928.

Some of the young chorus members of the Taibach Wesley Methodist Church production of the operetta Dulcinetta, 1951.

The Aconda dance band, a popular group of musicians in Skewen up to the early 1960s.

The chorus line of a Melyncrythan Amateur Operatic Society production, late 1950s.

The band of Neath's Salvation Army Corps, 1954.

Participants in a Nativity play at Orchard Place Baptist Church, Neath, 1962.

THE ENTERTAINERS

The choir of St Paul's Church, Aberavon, together with members of the congregation, late 1940s.

Members of the backstage crew of Briton Ferry Amateur Operatic Society during a production at the Gwyn Hall, early 1960s.

Neath tenor Allun Davies appearing on Hughie Green's TV talent show Opportunity Knocks which he won for a total of seven weeks, 1965.

The popular Margam Saints music group delight yet another Port Talbot audience during the early 1960s.

A scene from Neath Little Theatre's production of Goodnight Mrs Puffin, 1965.

The main cast members of Melyncrythan Amateur Operatic Society's production of Carousel, 1960.

Dancers who took part in Port Talbot Amateur Operatic Society's production of Rose Marie, 1969.

The Afan Paraders jazz band, Port Talbot, mid-1970s.

Members of Neath Male Voice Choir, with their accompanist at Sophia Gardens, Cardiff, 1966.

Resolven Male Voice Choir, with their conductor and accompanist, 1983.

The cast of Port Talbot Operatic Society's production of Carousel, 1978.

Participants in Cadoxton Opera Society's production of Verdi's Ernani which was staged at the Gwyn Hall, Neath, between April 15 and 19, 1997.

A band plays outside the Gwyn Hall, Neath, June 1990.

Members of the Masquerade Theatre Company entertaining an enthralled young audience during children's week at the Aberafan Shopping Centre, Port Talbot, 1980.

Young dancers entertain onlookers at Neath Castle grounds, September 1999.

Young members of the cast of Briton Ferry Amateur Operatic Society's production of the musical Blitz, October, 1995. This scene shows them sheltering in the Underground during a bombing raid.

Pupils of Central Infants School during a concert, June, 1983.

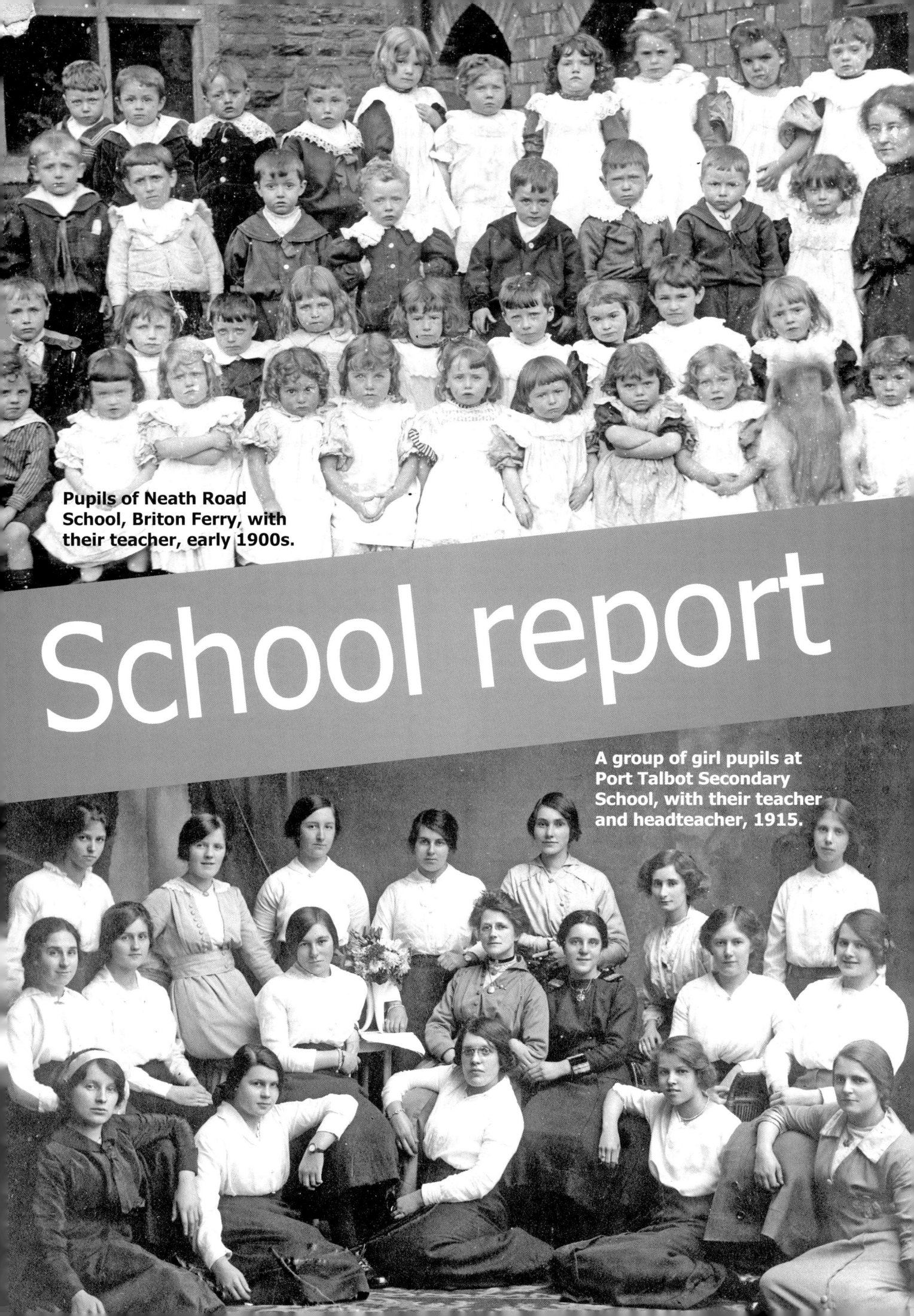

Pupils of Neath Road School, Briton Ferry, with their teacher, early 1900s.

School report

A group of girl pupils at Port Talbot Secondary School, with their teacher and headteacher, 1915.

Class 1 at Neath Road Infants School, Briton Ferry, 1930.

A stern faced teacher and headteacher with pupils of standards 5 and 6 at Eastern Boys School, Taibach, Port Talbot, 1911.

Pupils at Resolven Nursery School, one of the first to open in the Neath area, 1959.

Pupils at Cimla Infants school — the 'tin' school behind the fire station— with their Harvest Thanksgiving gifts, October 1947.

Standard 1b, Gnoll School, Neath, 1911. Their teacher and headteacher can be seen on the right.

Pupils and teachers of Sandfields Boys School, Port Talbot, with their teachers including Mr Sanderson, at the YMCA Hostel, Cold Knap, Barry, 1936.

SCHOOL REPORT

Pupils of Central Junior School, Port Talbot, mid-1930s.

Class 1b, Port Talbot Central Infants School, March 1927.

A class of pupils at Cwrt Sart Junior School, Briton Ferry, with their teacher Mr Williams, mid-1950s.

Mr Patrick O'Nei'ls class at St Joseph's Junior School for Boys, Aberavon, late 1950s.

Pupils at Trefelin Junior School, Velindre, Port Talbot, 1948.

Pupils of class 2C Neath Boys Grammar School, with their teacher, Mr Budge, 1950.

Pupils of Mountain Girls Junior School, Aberavon, 1956.

FORGOTTEN FACES OF **NEATH & PORT TALBOT**

Tywyn Junior School, Sandfields, Port Talbot, with teacher Miss Morgan, 1960.

A mixed class at Ynysmaerdy Primary School, Briton Ferry, with their teacher, 1955.

SCHOOL REPORT

Standard 5, Alderman Davies Girls Junior School, Neath, 1954.

Pupils of Baglan Junior School with their teacher Mr Perkins and headteacher Miss Richards, 1960.

Pupils at Crynallt Junior School, Cimla, Neath, 1958.

A class at Trefelin Primary School, Port Talbot, with their teacher 1960.

SCHOOL REPORT

Children of Ambleside Nursery, George Street, Port Talbot, 1967.

A class at Gnoll Junior School, Neath 1959.

Pupils at Baglan Junior School with their teacher, Mr Jenkins, 1970.

Resolven Nursery Class, 1958 with teachers Hilda Davies and Margaret Williams.

SCHOOL REPORT

A class at Bryncoch Church in Wales Infants School, with their teacher, 1965.

Students and their tutor at Margam Technical College, Port Talbot, 1971.

FORGOTTEN FACES OF **NEATH & PORT TALBOT**

Pupils at Groes Primary School, Bertha Road, Margam, shortly after its official opening, July 10, 1973. The original school, along with Groes Village had been demolished to make way for the M4 motorway.

SCHOOL REPORT

Pupils at Park Nursery, Port Talbot, celebrate St David's Day, 1981.

Some of the pupils and staff at Melin County Junior School in its centenary year, 1973. Even the school's two popular lollipop road crossing attendants are included.

Form 6A Science, Dyffryn Comprehensive School, Port Talbot, with biology master Derek Morgan, 1983.

Teacher David Williams with his class at Cefn Saeson Comprehensive School, Cimla, Neath, 1983.

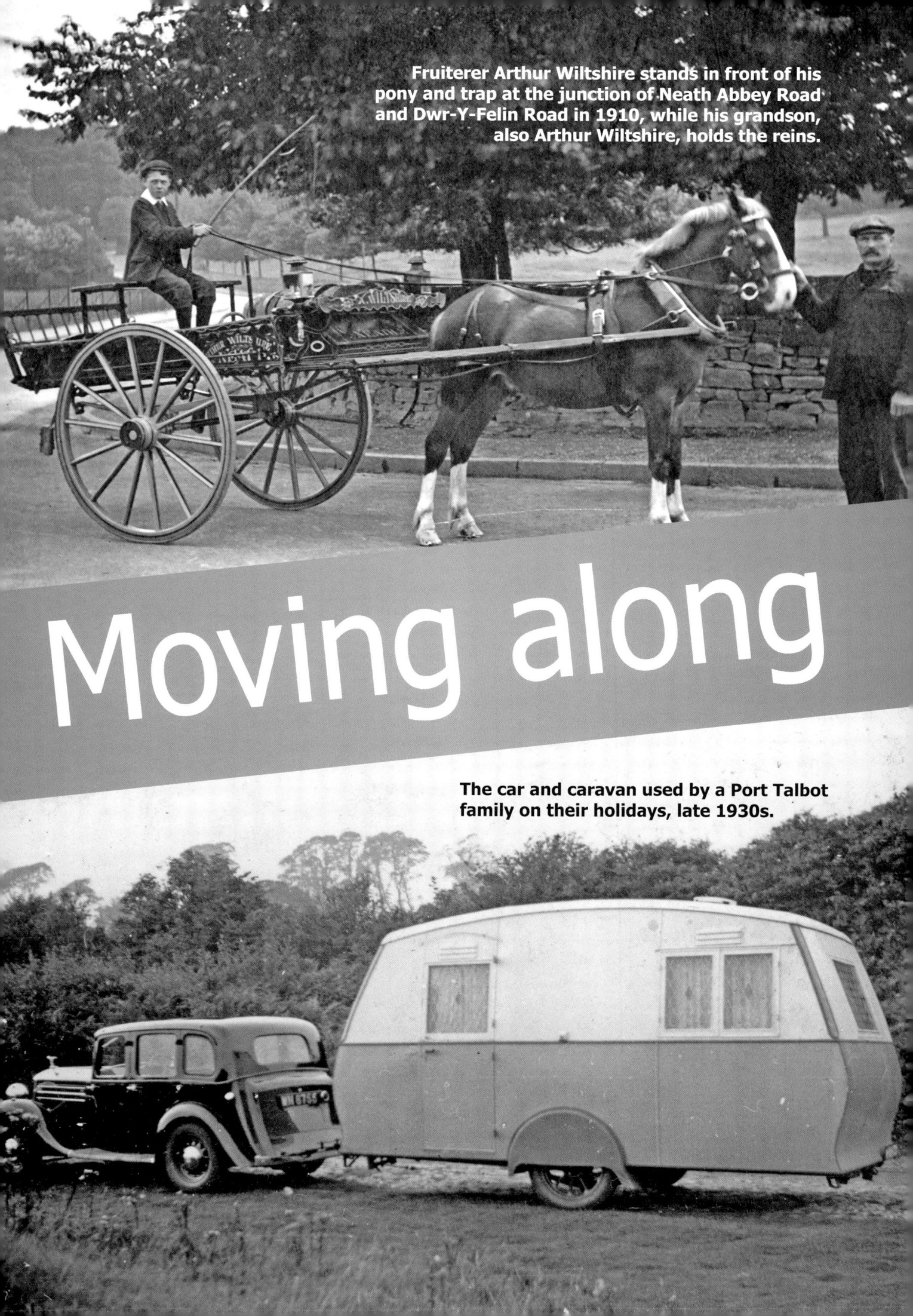

Fruiterer Arthur Wiltshire stands in front of his pony and trap at the junction of Neath Abbey Road and Dwr-Y-Felin Road in 1910, while his grandson, also Arthur Wiltshire, holds the reins.

Moving along

The car and caravan used by a Port Talbot family on their holidays, late 1930s.

A Neath family enjoy a day out by car to Nottage, Porthcawl, 1925.

William Evans on his motorcycle in Pontrhydyfen, during the early 1930s.

The sand dredger, Francis Gilbertson, was a familiar sight at Port Talbot Docks and the mouth of the River Afan during the early 1950s.

MOVING ALONG

This delivery van pictured with its driver was used for deliveries by the Afan Valley Modern Co-operative Society's store at 47 Pelly Street, Cwmavon during the 1920s.

A young mechanic sits astride the mudguard of a Maudslay bus at the Western Welsh Omnibus Company's Cadoxton Road depot, Neath, mid-1930s.

The vessel MV Altmark beached on Margam Sands, Port Talbot, June, 12, 1960.

The Westen Welsh bus company garage at Cadoxton, Neath, with an AEC Regal, LT1 Leyland Lion bus and a Wolseley 9 car owned by depot manager Mr AC Willett, 1930s.

MOVING ALONG

An engineer stands alongside an AEC bus he had been working on at the Cadoxton Road, Neath, depot of the Western Welsh Omnibus Company, mid-1930s.

A Port Talbot woman with the car that towed the family caravan on holidays during the late 1930s.

A steam-hauled, two carriage, local passenger train at Neath General railway station on February 29, 1964.

The Dutch tanker, Michael Svenden, is buffeted by rough seas after running aground near the old wooden pier at Aberavon beach, 1957.

Efforts are made to recover a British Oxygen Company lorry that veered off the road and plunged into the River Afan below Newbridge Road bridge, Aberavon, in the early 1950s.

An ocean-going iron ore carrier squeezes into the lock gates at Port Talbot Docks, with the silhouette of the steelworks behind, mid-1950s.

Freight meets passenger as two trains pass on the level crossing east of Port Talbot station, 1984.

MOVING ALONG

A local passenger train heads through Resolven on its way to Neath with the backs of houses in Rheola Avenue to the left, 1950s.

The driver of this van, owned by Dewi R Phillips Ltd, had some explaining to do after it went out of control and careered into a roadside garden at Afan Valley Road, Cimla, Neath, mid-1960s.

To most they were still Thomas Bros, but the sign on the side of this Baglan-bound bus at Station Road, Port Talbot in 1971, said South Wales, the fleet into which the town-based passenger carrying operation had been absorbed.

A loaded coal train pulls away from Onllwyn Washery, at the head of the Dulais Valley, in 1987 leaving a gathering of empty wagons looking forlorn in the sidings alongside.

A Creamline Services bus makes a solitary presence in the Victoria Gardens bus station at Neath after heavy snow in early 1983. The journey ahead would take it up the steep climb of Cimla Road.

A South Wales Transport bus awaits its duty on the route to Tonmawr from Victoria Gardens bus station Neath in the mid-1980s.

A bulk iron ore carrier berthed at Port Talbot tidal harbour, 1978.

A Creamline Services, bus pulls its way up Y Berllan hill on the Glannant Estate, Cimla, late 1986.

The pleasure barge Enfys, moored on the Neath Canal at Resolven, mid-1990s.

Passengers aboard a paddle steamer bound for Ilfracombe from Briton Ferry, 1933.

Break time

Crowds on the seafront at Aberavon Beach, early 1900s.

The lower Gnoll Pond in the mid-1920s when it was Neath Corporation's swimming pool. The cubicles were for changing into swim wear. On summer days the location was often packed with swimmers.

Crowds throng Aberavon Beach, on a hot summer's day in the late 1950s.

Donkeys at rest between giving rides to visitors at Aberavon Beach, mid-1950s.

Staff of the Prudential Assurance office, Neath on a day out to Bristol, 1933.

A Port Talbot family on a touring caravan holiday, late 1930s. Tents, tables and deckchairs were all necessities if the job was to be done properly, as the picture below confirms.

A party of friends and neighbours from Skewen on an outing, mid-1950s.

Resolven residents and their friends on a trip to Blackpool organised by Mrs Nellie Roberts, early 1950s.

A group of Tonmawr residents on a trip to Blackpool, early 1950s.

Pupils of Alderman Davies' Church in Wales School, Neath, with teachers and parents outside the town's railway station prepare to set off for an excursion to Bristol Zoo, 1958.

Women of Bethania Chapel Sisterhood, Port Talbot, all set for an outing, early 1960s.

BREAK TIME

Friends and neighbours from Margam during a 1952 trip to Blackpool.

Tonmawr RFC 1958-59 with officials and supporters on a tour of Huddersfield.

FORGOTTEN FACES OF **NEATH & PORT TALBOT**

Members of Neath Red Cross having a relaxing time at Aberavon Beach, late 1950s.

A family enjoys one of the attractions of Neath Fair in a busy Wind Street, September, 1962.

The Afan Lido Swimming Pool, 1966.

BREAK TIME

With headscarves to keep their new hairdo's intact these women employees of the Briton Ferry and Neath Co-operative Society enjoy a day out at Weston-Super-Mare, late 1950s.

Watery hi-jinks at the Afan Lido before it became the Aquadome, March 1985.

Members of the Sisterhood of Wesley Hall, Port Talbot, prepare for a day's outing to Blenheim Palace, Oxfordshire, June 1961.

Some of those who took part in the Holiday Club organised by members of Wesley Methodist Church, Taibach, at Margam Park, Port Talbot, 1993.

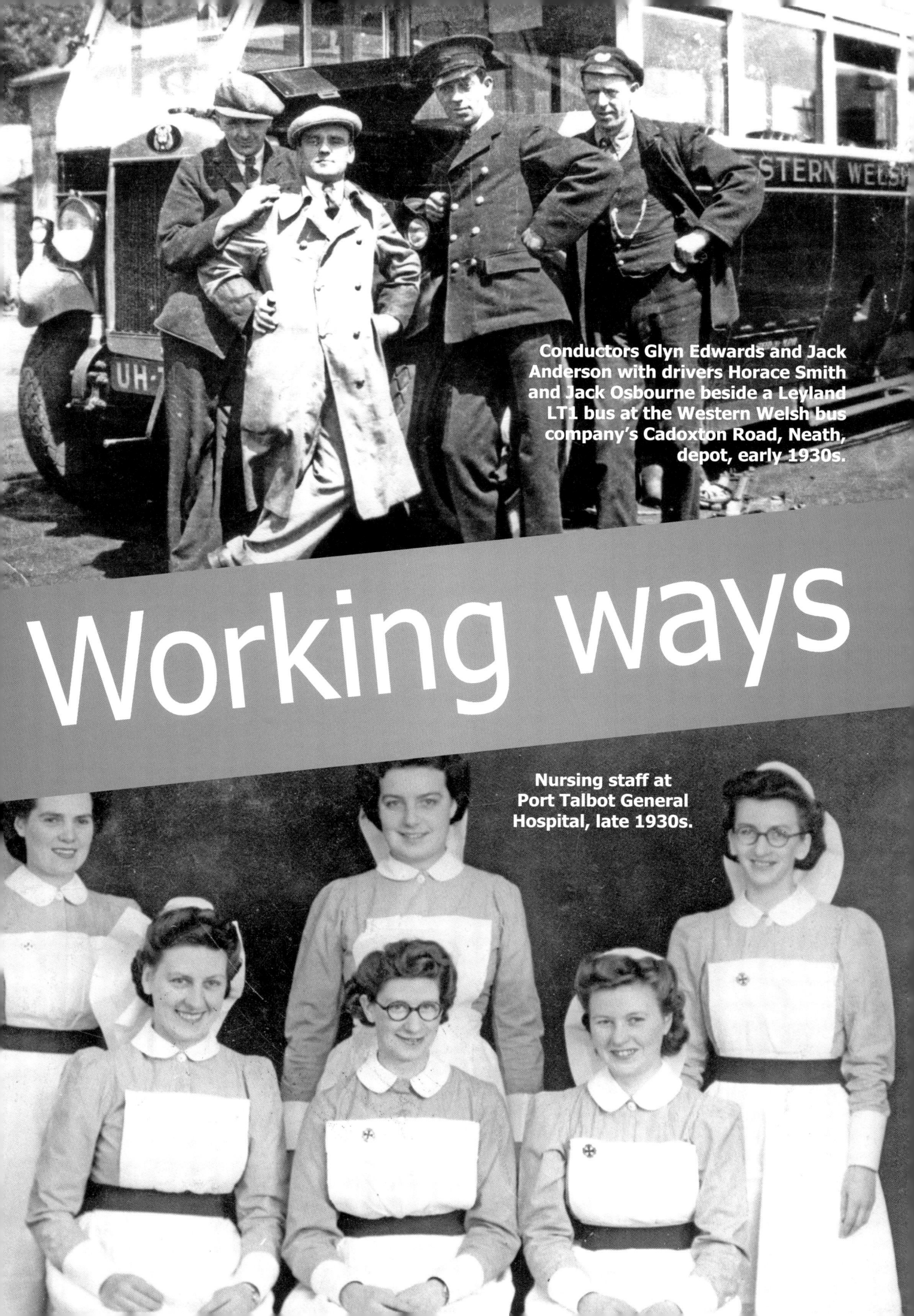

Conductors Glyn Edwards and Jack Anderson with drivers Horace Smith and Jack Osbourne beside a Leyland LT1 bus at the Western Welsh bus company's Cadoxton Road, Neath, depot, early 1930s.

Working ways

Nursing staff at Port Talbot General Hospital, late 1930s.

Pithead winding gear and ancillary buildings at Glyncastle Colliery, Resolven, early 1900s.

Women teachers at Trefelin School, Velindre, Port Talbot, 1946-48.

WORKING WAYS

A group of employees in the heavy bar mill at Port Talbot steelworks, late 1920s.

Fitters at the Western Welsh bus company's Cadoxton Road garage, Neath. From the left: Rhys Thomas, Billy Whittle, Dilwyn Thomas, Billie Davies and Harry Humphries, mid-1930s.

Staff at Cwrt Sart railway station, Briton Ferry, 1910. The site is currently occupied by a series of industrial buildings.

Contractors and machinery employed on pile driving at the Steel Company of Wales Port Talbot works, 1950. The former Margam tinworks can be seen in the background.

This gang of Great Western Railway platelayers were working on one of the valley lines out of Port Talbot, late 1940s.

The Vale of Neath Brewery, Cadoxton Road, Cadoxton, Neath, early 1960s.

Port Talbot Docks, with the steelworks alongside, 1930s.

Red Jacket copper works, near Llandarcy, 1930s.

Drawing the first ingot from the soakers at the Abbey slab mill, Port Talbot, November 1950.

Employees of the Albion steel works, Briton Ferry, 1930s.

Staff of the David Phillips bakery, 22 Queen Street, Neath, enjoy a moment of fun with a dog, 1931.

Teaching staff at Tywyn Primary School, Port Talbot, 1953.

Briton Ferry Steel works, 1950.

The landlady and barmaids at the Vivian Hotel, Aberavon, 1961.

The British Hydrocarbon Company's works at the western end of Aberavon Beach, 1963.

An aerial view of the sprawling Reynolds TI Aluminium works at Rheola, Neath Valley, later British Aluminium, mid-1950s.

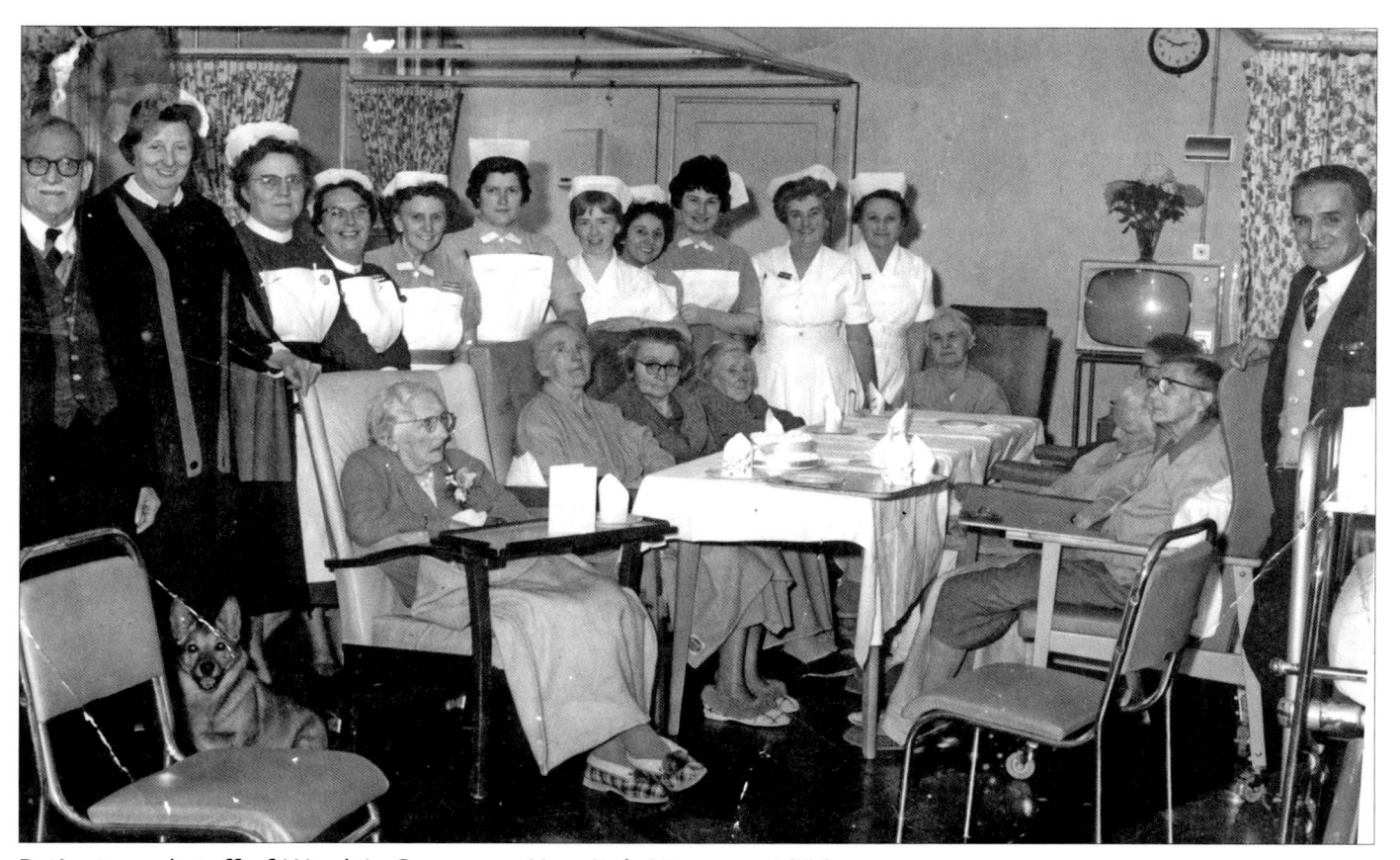

Patients and staff of Ward 1, Groeswen Hospital, Margam, 1966.

The librarian and staff of Neath Library during the late 1940s.

The BP Baglan Bay chemical complex, viewed from Maes-Ty-Canol, Baglan, 1984.

WORKING WAYS

The scene after the demolition, in the mid-1980s, of a huge gasometer that was part of the British Steel Corporation's Port Talbot works. It had stood for many years near the town's railway station.

Women at work in the Neath Steel Sheet and Galvanising works, early 1950s.

Dyffryn Rhondda Colliery, in the Afan Valley, mid-1950s.

Serving petrol at Huxtable's Garage, Baglan, 1952.

Workers at the High Duty Alloys works, Briton Ferry, having a break from their labours, 1964.

Clerical, engineering and scientific staff of the EM Edwards gas works taken on the day of the Investiture of Prince Charles as Prince of Wales, July, 1969.

FORGOTTEN FACES OF **NEATH & PORT TALBOT**

Staff of Crynallt Junior School, Cimla, Neath, late 1960s.

Colliers and stable hands with pit ponies at Goytre, Port Talbot, mid-1950s.

Parents and children from The Green, Neath, celebrate the Coronation of Queen Elizabeth II, June, 1953.

Party time

A street party organised by residents of Gwyn Terrace, often referred to as Skittle Alley because of its narrow width, and Water Street, Aberavon, to celebrate the Festival of Britain, 1951.

Festival of Britain celebrations at Rhanallt Street, Margam, 1951.

Employees of the Pearl Assurance Company's Port Talbot office at their annual dinner, 1953.

PARTY TIME

Residents of Florence Street, Neath, at the street party they held to celebrate the Coronation of Queen Elizabeth II, June 2, 1953. They are, from left: Mrs D John, sister of actor William Squire; M Spreadborough, Mrs G Griffiths, Mrs J Harris and a neighbour.

Residents of Angel Street, Aberavon, at the party they held to celebrate the Festival of Britain, 1951.

The residents of Allister Street, Neath, celebrating the Festival of Britain, 1951.

Residents of Cove Road and Vivian Park Drive, Sandfields, Port Talbot, during their street party to celebrate the Coronation of Queen Elizabeth II, June, 1953.

Residents of Farm Drive, Sandfields, Port Talbot, during the street party they held to celebrate the Coronation of Queen Elizabeth II, 1953.

A street party in Goytre Crescent, Goytre, Port Talbot, to mark the Coronation of Queen Elizabeth II, June 1953.

Members of Resolven Army Cadets and their guests at a special dinner and dance they held, mid-1950s.

Staff of the BP Refinery, Llandarcy at one of the popular dinner dances they held at the Brangwyn Hall, Swansea on a regular basis in the 1960s.

Some of the residents of Lingfield Avenue, Sandfields, Port Talbot during the street party they held to celebrate the Coronation of Queen Elizabeth II, June 1953.

Staff at Neath General Post Office at their Christmas party, 1955.

Employees of the FW Woolworth store, Station Road, Port Talbot, during their Christmas party, early 1950s.

PARTY TIME

Children of employees of the ICI Carbide plant at Margam, during their Christmas party, 1957.

Guests at a retirement party for Mr Henry, manager of the National Assistance Board, Neath 1965.

Staff of the DHSS Supplementary Benefits Office at the Drill Hall, Port Talbot during their Christmas party, 1978.

Residents of Bwlch Road, Cimla, celebrate the Investiture of the Prince of Wales, with a street party, July 1969.

A group of family and friends during a 21st birthday party celebration at Antolin's Ros a Mar Rooms, Port Talbot, 1968.

Members of the ladies section of Aberavon Green Stars Rugby Club enjoy an evening out at Antolin's restaurant, early 1970s.

A presentation at the diamond wedding celebration of Mr and Mrs H Harrison Neath, 1967.

A group of Margam railway workers and their wives during a Christmas night out, 1962.

A gathering of Cadoxton, Neath, children celebrate the Investiture of the Prince of Wales, July, 1969.

A group of members at Trefelin Working Men's Club, Velindre, Port Talbot, 1974.

PARTY TIME

Crynant Welfare Club ladies committee during their fancy dress celebrations to mark the Investiture of the Prince of Wales, July 1969.

Fancy dress was the order of the day for children at this street party in Pine Valley Close, Cwmavon, held to celebrate the Silver Jubilee of Queen Elizabeth II, July 1977. Mayor of Afan, Graham Jones is in the centre.

Disney-style fun during a street party to commemorate the wedding of Prince Charles and Lady Diana, Mayfield Street, Port Talbot, 1981.

Women of Orchard Place Baptist Church, Orchard Street, Neath, celebrate the birthday of Miss Rene Sherwood a well-known retired headteacher in the town, early 1970s. Miss Sherwood was also a Deacon of Orchard Place Church.

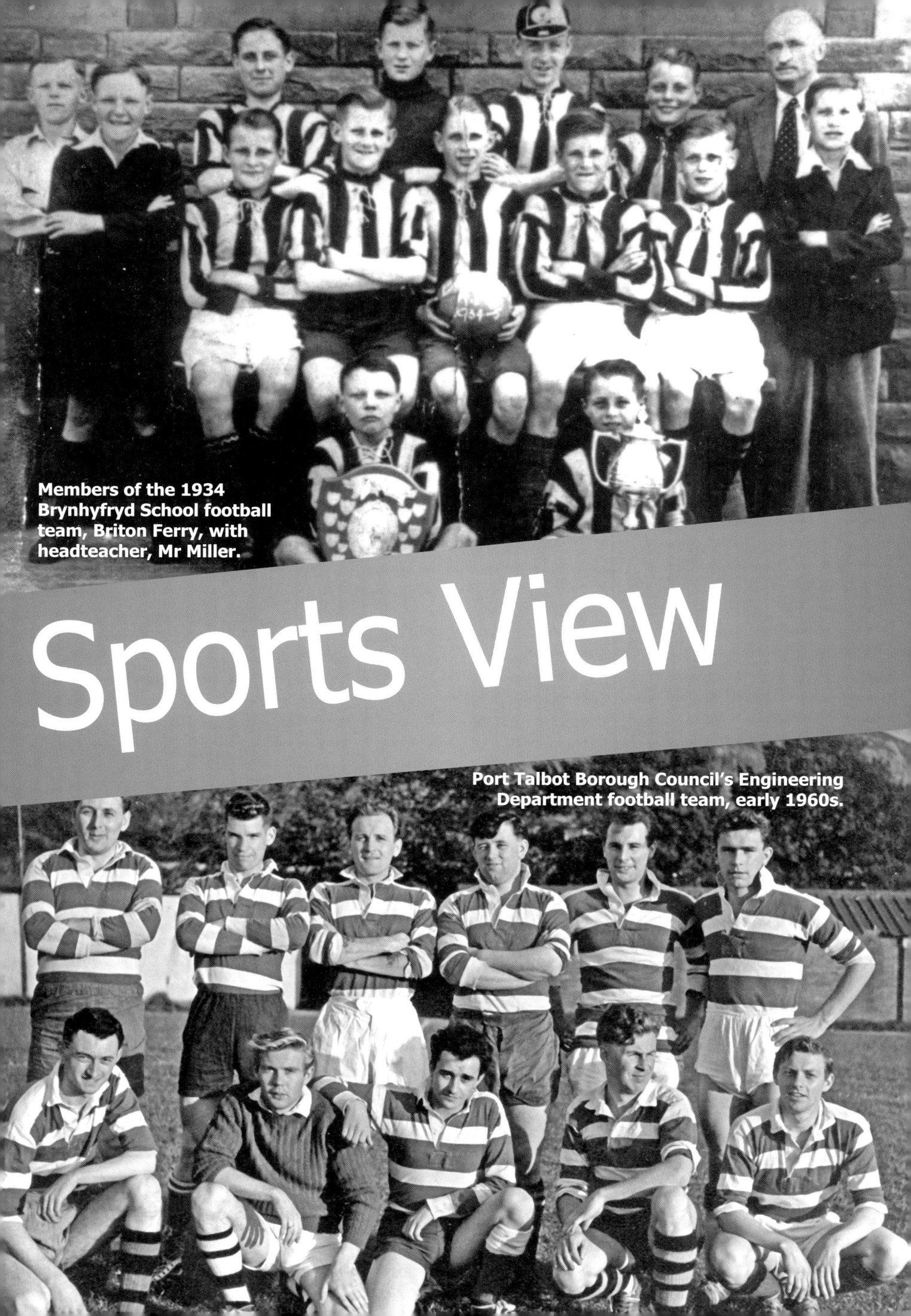

Members of the 1934 Brynhyfryd School football team, Briton Ferry, with headteacher, Mr Miller.

Sports View

Port Talbot Borough Council's Engineering Department football team, early 1960s.

Neath RFC's 1907-08 squad with club officials at the Gnoll Ground.

Players and officials of Taibach RFC, 1947-48.

The senior cricket XI of Eastern School, Taibach, Port Talbot, display the shield they received as winners of the Roath challenge competition in 1936. Headteacher WJ Samuel is to the left of the shield and teacher FS Elliot is to the right.

Members of Briton Ferry Bowls Club display the spoils of a successful competition during the 1930s.

Glanafan Grammar School Under XV 1951-52 with their sports teacher and headteacher.

Officers and committee members of Neath Golf Club pictured at the official opening of their new clubhouse, Thursday, June 6, 1935.

Neath Post Office cricket team and officials, 1936.

Resolven Bowls Club, winners of the Neath and District League, 1939.

A group of Neath RFC players and officials during a 1930s tour.

Members of the Tirmorfa School rugby team, Sandfields, Port Talbot, 1960.

Sidney Davies, an enthusiastic member of Port Talbot Wheelers cycling club, with trophies he won in 1950.

Sandfields Comprehensive School's Under 13s rugby team with teacher and headteacher, 1960.

Briton Ferry Steel Cricket Club, winners of the South Wales and Monmouthshire league and Dan Radcliffe Cup, 1939. The group includes players and officials.

Players and officials of Aberavon Harlequins Rugby Club, 1964.

Neath Post Office Bowls Team, 1950.

Briton Ferry Town Cricket team with officials and perhaps three of the women without whose support — and cucumber sandwiches — they couldn't have functioned, 1950s.

Athletes from Sandfields Comprehensive School, Port Talbot, after a day's competition at Maindy Stadium, Cardiff, June 1964.

An Aberavon Boys Club football team at Victoria Road ground, Aberavon before taking part in a local league cup final game, 1966.

Mount Pleasant Albion football team, Melincrythan, Neath, 1950s.

SPORTS VIEW

Members of the Melincrythan cricket team, Neath, mid-1950s.

Aberavon Green Stars rugby squad, 1967-68, season.

Members of Neath British Legion club darts team during a presentation evening, 1969.

Members of the Town Hall Barbarians, five-a-side football squad with colleagues and the Mayor of Port Talbot, William Lewis, 1967.

Sandfields Comprehensive School's 2nd XV rugby team, 1968-1969.

Neath RFC's Centenary Year squad, 1971-1972. The club were WRU Challenge Cup finalists in their celebratory season.

FORGOTTEN FACES OF **NEATH & PORT TALBOT**

A young lad strikes it lucky at Aberavon beach. His trip there coincided with the first Welsh Rugby Union squad training session at the Afan Lido. He came away with these fascinating photographs of stars of the day and some autographs to boot, early 1970s.

Members of the BP Llandarcy refinery Golf Society, 1979.

Ynysfach Primary School netball team, Resolven, 1985.

The Mumbles to Aberavon row, organised by Port Talbot Round Table, 1970s.

Members of a Briton Ferry Steel Bowls Club team, early 1980s.

Men and women take part in an archery competition at BP's Llandarcy refinery sports club fields, 1995.